All About

Elon Musk

Elon Musk Biography Children's Book for Kids

(With Bonus! Coloring Pages and Videos)

By All About Books

Before You Go Any Further, Get Your FREE Gift! (Worth $67)

Never Fear "The Call" from the School or the Hospital Again!

How to Effectively Communicate With Your Child About *Safety* in a <u>Fun Way!</u>

Did you know if children are not taught properly about safety at a young age, it can potentially lead to reckless, dangerous behaviors even when they become a teenager or an adult?

Never fear "the call" from the school or the hospital with this comprehensive video course!

It'll teach you how to communicate effectively with your young ones about safety without boring them!

(Limited-Time FREE Gift)

Get It Before It Expires Here:

https://allaboutbookseries.com/freegift/

Table of Contents

Disclaimer and Note to Readers:

This book is an unofficial tribute book to Elon Musk from a fan to support his legacy.

The information in this book is provided for educational and entertainment purposes only.

The information in this book has been compiled from reliable sources. It is accurate to the best of the author's knowledge; however, the author cannot guarantee its accuracy and validity and cannot be held liable for any errors or omissions.

If you use the information contained in this book, you agree that the author is free from and not liable for any damages, costs, and expenses, including any legal fees, potentially resulting from applying any of the information provided by this guide.

The disclaimer applies to any damages or injury caused by the use and application, whether directly or indirectly, of any advice or information presented, whether for breach of contract, tort, neglect, personal injury, criminal intent, or under any other cause of action. You agree to accept all risks of using the information presented inside this book.

If an individual cites this publication as the source of information, it does not imply that the author or publisher endorse the individual or organization's knowledge. This book is an unofficial fan tribute and has not been approved or endorsed by Elon Musk or his associates.

Maurizio Pesce from Milan, Italia CC by 2.0

Introduction to Elon Musk

When we talk about electric cars and space travel, the first thing that comes to mind is Tesla and Elon Musk.

Elon Musk is referred to as a deity in Silicon Valley. One of the reasons is his ability and willingness to tackle things that other people see as impossible. He has seen problems and attacked them all his life, no matter how impossible they seemed.

He is the wealthiest man in the world, but there's a lot of mystery about him. So many people think he's an Alien. Do you think so too? So, who exactly is this guy? What makes him so unique? How did he become one of the most influential people in the world? What is his story? Don't be in a hurry; I'll be spilling what I discovered about this genius who might be an Alien. I'm joking but keep reading.

Elon Musk is the founder and CEO of SpaceX. He is an investor, CEO, and product architect of Tesla, Inc. He is the founder of The Boring Company and a co-founder of Neuralink and OpenAI. He co-founded the online payment platform PayPal.

According to Forbes real-time billionaire's list and Bloomberg billionaires index, Elon Musk is the wealthiest person in the world. His net worth as of January 2022 is estimated at around US$243 billion. He is the father of six sons.

Elon Musk started building his empire in the late 1990s. Musk and his younger brother sold their software company, which provided city business guides to newspapers. He didn't stop at that. He went further and invested his money into a new company, "X.com," which promised to cause a revolution in payments, and it did. You might know the company now as PayPal. Elon Musk sold the company to eBay and took his profits to invest once again. He set up SpaceX with the mission to help humans live on other planets. He has plans to colonize Mars.

He set up Tesla to work on environmental problems that come with vehicles. He plans that all vehicles, including trains, will go electric except for rockets.

The billionaire has suffered losses, especially in dealing with SpaceX and Tesla's companies. Still, he came through everything stronger. That's why he's standing tall as the richest man on earth.

Musk is also famous for making many controversial statements that are unscientific. He spread misinformation about the COVID-19 pandemic and received criticism from experts for his other views on artificial intelligence, cryptocurrency, and public transport.

Who is Elon Musk?

http://allaboutbookseries.com/WhoIsElonMusk

Elon Musk's Early Childhood

Elon Reeve Musk was born in South Africa on June 28, 1971, to a South African father and a Canadian mother. Engineering didn't just start in the family. His father, Erol Musk, was an electromechanical engineer, pilot, sailor, consultant, and property developer who was once a half-owner of a Zambian emerald mine near Lake Tanganyika. His mother, Maye Musk (neè Halderman), was a model and dietician.

Musk has two younger siblings: his brother Kimbal and his sister Tosca. He was named after his great grandfather, John Elon Halderman. As a child, Elon Musk was frequently teased about his name.

One could say Elon Musk was similar to his mum. Maye Musk grew up with a love for maths and science. She was considered a nerd. When she was fifteen, people began to notice her beauty, so she was enrolled in a modelling school. She modeled into her sixties and even appeared on the cover of Elle and in one of Beyonce's music videos.

While growing up, Elon Musk was an energetic child, and he picked up things quickly. However, he would randomly drift into his world, and nothing anyone did would distract him.

"You could do jumping jacks right beside Musk or yell at him, and he would not even notice. He kept right on thinking, and those around him judged that he was either rude or weird.

"I do think Elon was always a little different but in a nerdy way," Maye said. *"It didn't endear him to his peers."*

Elon Musk's condition was more about how his mind worked rather than his hearing. Doctors thought he was deaf in his early childhood because he would randomly drift off, so they advised that his adenoid gland be removed to help his hearing, but nothing happened. He still drifts off sometimes as an adult.

At the age of five and six, he could successfully block out external distractions just to focus on a task. Part of this stemmed from the graphic way his mind works. He could see images in his mind. Elon has likened his mind to a graphic chip that lets him see things and replicate them.

Another thing about Elon Musk is that he had a compulsion to read from a young age. *"It was not unusual for him to read ten hours a day,"* said Kimbal. *"If it was the weekend, he could go through two books in a day."*

Whenever the family went on one of their numerous shopping excursions, they would realize that Elon had gone missing mid-trip. Maye or Kimbal would often pop into the nearest bookstore to find Elon somewhere near the back, sitting on the floor and reading in one of his trancelike states.

When Elon got older, he would go to the bookstore after school and stay there till his parents returned. He ran out of books at one point, and then he started to read encyclopedias. In fourth grade, he read through two sets of encyclopedias.

Elon had a photographic memory, so he became a walking fact machine. *"At the dinner table, Tosca would wonder aloud about the distance from Earth to the Moon. Elon would spit out the exact measurement at perigee and apogee. If we had a question, Tosca would always say, 'Just ask genius boy,'"* Maye said. *"We could ask him about anything. He just remembered it."*

He also believed that people liked to hear the flaws in their thinking, so he often spat facts in an abrasive manner, which made him appear the classic know-all. Due to this, kids would always say, *"Elon, we are not playing with you anymore."*

As a result, Elon didn't have friends. His siblings Kimbal and Tosca would bring friends home while Elon wouldn't. It was evident that he wanted to play with other kids, but he was awkward. So, Maye would tell Kimbal and Tosca to include him, and they would always reply, *"But Mom, he's not fun."*

While growing up, Elon Musk was bullied, and he often kept to himself. He was bullied so bad he got hospitalized for a week after a group of boys threw him down the stairs.

Question to Ponder: How do you think bullying affected Elon Musk? Have you ever been bullied or witnessed somebody getting bullied? How did you feel?

Musk grew up in a wealthy home. He mentioned that "We had so much money at times we couldn't even close our safe."

At age ten, Musk developed an interest in computing and video games, and he learned how to code using a manual. When he was twelve years old, he created a video game, "Blaster," using the BASIC program, which he sold for $500.

The games hinted at Elon Musk's character. The source code for the game was published by South Africa's trade publication "PC and Office technology." It was a science fiction-inspired game, where the player had to destroy an alien space machine carrying hydrogen bombs and status beam machines. The game made good use of animation.

While the game did not shine as a marvel in computer science, it was better than what many twelve-year-olds were making.

Question to Ponder: How do you think Elon Musk felt when he made his first game, and it was published? How would you feel if any of your work got published by a reputable magazine company?

Elon Musk grew up in the apartheid version of South Africa. Apartheid is racial discrimination, where whites are seen as superior to blacks.

Question to Ponder: How do you think apartheid affected Elon Musk?

He grew up in Pretoria, and his childhood was characterized by violence. Whites and blacks clashed; the different black tribes also clashed. He was just four years old after the Soweto uprising, which led to the death of many black students while they fought against white decrees from the government. There were many racist policies in South Africa then, which influenced his decision to leave South Africa.

About his childhood, Elon Musk mentioned, *"When I was a child, there's one thing I said: 'I never want to be alone.'"*

OnInnovation Interview: Elon Musk by OnInnovation is marked with CC BY-ND 2.0

Elon Musk's Education

Elon Musk attended Waterkloof House Preparatory School and Bryanston High School and later graduated from Pretoria Boys High School in South Africa.

After high school, Elon Musk decided to migrate to the United States of America for better economic activities. Elon Musk had to get a Canadian passport through his mother's side of the family to easily migrate to the United States. While processing his documentation, he attended the University of Pretoria for five months. As a result, he avoided mandatory service in the South African military. During this period in South Africa, there was apartheid. Elon Musk was unwilling to support the apartheid government.

His documentation was successful, and he moved to Canada in June 1989. Elon worked odd jobs at a farm and lumber mill and lived with a second cousin during his first year in Canada.

By the following year, 1990, Elon Musk got admission to Queen's University in Ontario. After two years, he transferred to the University of Pennsylvania, where he graduated with a Bachelor of Science degree in Economics. He stayed for a second Bachelors of Science degree in physics.

During his two years at Queen's University, he met his first wife, Justine Wilson, and tried to woo her.

In the summer of 1994, he began two internships in Silicon Valley. One was at an energy storage start-up Pinnacle Research Institute, which researched electrolytic ultracapacitors for energy storage, and at the Palo Alto-based start-up Rocket Science Games. He also tried to get a job at Netscape, but he never got a reply to his inquiries.

A year later, he was accepted to the Ph.D. program of material science at Stanford University. He dropped out after two days, deciding to join the internet boom to build an internet start-up.

As an immigrant in America, Elon Musk experienced the country as the land of opportunities. He experienced his dreams coming true.

Elon Musk by Thomas Hawk is marked with CC BY-NC 2.0

Elon Musk's Business Career

In 1995, Elon Musk launched his software company Zip2. He partnered with his brother, Kimbal, and a friend, Greg Kouri. The trio used funds from an Angel investment company to do this. The software company was located in a rented space in Palo Alto. In the company's early days, their father gave them $28 thousand to support them, but after paying for the office, they became broke. Elon Musk and Kimbal could not afford an apartment, so they slept on the couch of the rented office and showered at the YMCA. The toilet would often act up. They shared one computer. During this period, the website would be live during the day, while Elon would code at night.

They developed a city guide for the newspaper publishing industry, with maps, directions, and yellow pages. Genius, when you think about it.

This idea had come during one of his internships at Silicon Valley. A salesperson from Yellow Pages had come to pitch about an online listing to compliment the listing of companies on yellow pages.

Yellow Pages is a kind of telephone directory with listings of businesses like handymen, lawyers, etc. It used to be printed in yellow on newspaper material. These days, you can find the Yellow Pages online.

It was so obvious that the man didn't know much about the internet and how it could be used to find businesses. Anyway, the pitch was terrible, but it got Elon Musk thinking. So, he reached out to Kimbal about how they could put businesses online for the first time.

Question to Ponder: Have you ever gotten inspiration from someone's idea? How do you think Elon Musk felt about putting businesses online?

Elon Musk saw that there was a wealth of opportunity on the internet, and businesses would want to utilize the internet. This led to the creation of Zip2, which was a way to create a platform for business owners, especially because so many of them did not know how to go on the internet. The brothers tried to convince hairdressers and restaurants to use their platform. Elon Musk would explain using pizza. He would say, *"everyone deserves the right to know the location of their closest pizza parlor and the turn-by-turn directions to get there."*

Even though the company's goal was tethered to information technology, they had to use the old door-to-door salesman method to convince businesses of the benefits of the internet.

Kimbal would meet up with people while Elon Musk did the coding. Elon Musk acquired a cheap license to a database of business listings in the Bay Area that would give a business's name and address. He then contacted Navteq, a company that had spent hundreds of millions of dollars to create digital maps and directions that could be used in early GPS navigation-style devices and struck a masterful bargain.

"We called them up, and they gave us the technology for free," said Kimbal.

Elon Musk combined both databases to get a fundamental system for their software up and running.

Greg Kouri was a Canadian businessman who had worked in real estate. He was familiar with business, so he acted as a mentor for the group. He would often calm Elon Musk and put things in context for him.

"Greg is one of the few people that Elon would listen to and had a way of putting things in context for him."

He used to referee fights between the team.

Question to Ponder: Do you have anybody who calms you down on bad days? How does it feel?

In 1996, the venture capital firm Mohr Davidow Ventures heard about a couple of South African boys trying to make a Yellow Pages for the Internet and met with the Musk brothers.

Elon Musk was really passionate in his presentation. He pitched the company excellently, and the investors left impressed with his energy. Mohr Davidow invested $3 million into the company.

The company used the funds to change its name from Global Link to Zip2. (The idea being zip to here, zip to there.)

They moved to a larger office at 390 Cambridge Avenue in Palo Alto and hired talented engineers. The engineers brought a more structured look to the company. They also rewrote most of the codes. Since Elon Musk was a self-taught coder, many of the codes he wrote could actually go haywire for no reason.

The change also affected the business strategy of the company. Zip2 advanced its course of business from focusing just on the Bay Area to have a national scope. At the time of this change, the company had built one of the best direction systems on the Web.

The company also shifted its main focus. It went from selling its service door-to-door to creating a software package that could be sold to newspapers, which would, in turn, build their own directories for real estate, auto dealers, and classifieds. The newspapers did not realize early enough that the internet would impact their businesses positively. Sites like Craigslist were online, and the newspapers knew they had to do things on the internet. However, Zip2's software offered them a quick way of getting online without needing to develop all their own technology from scratch. They gave an additional $50 million in funding.

The company had contracts with The New York Times and the Chicago Tribune.

Working on this start-up gave Elon Musk a new kind of self-confidence. He was no longer the kid that bullies used to pick on to get a response; he was a self-assured man who was in control.

Elon Musk had plans to be the company's CEO, but the plans failed as the board squashed it. They put Elon as the chief technology officer and hired Richard Sorkin as the CEO. While Elon Musk agreed to the whole agreement, he later resented giving up the company.

Question to Ponder: How would you feel if a position you wanted was given to another person?

The founders of Zip2, the musk brothers, and Kouri persuaded the board of directors to abandon plans for a merger with CitySearch.

Initially, the plan to merge with CitySearch was to bring about $300 million to the company. Elon Musk supported this deal, but there were some dissonant clauses indicating the differences in their approach to technology and product development. The deal fell through, and both Richard Sorkin and Elon Musk suffered a lot of backlashes. Musk was no longer in the race for chairman as the board gave Derek Proudian, a venture capitalist with Mohr Davidow, the chairman title.

After the deal with CitySearch went west, Zip2 was losing a lot of money. Also, Microsoft launched in the market, and it didn't seem like the company could compete with them. Then Compaq happened.

Compaq later bought the company for $307 million in February 1999. Elon Musk received $22 million for his 7 percent share.

As soon as the company was sold, Elon moved on to his next project.

Elon Musk - The Summit 2013 by Heisenberg Media is marked with CC BY 2.0

X.com

In 1999, after the sale of Zip2 was concluded, Elon Musk decided to form a new company. For his next company, he wanted to explore a sector with money. He felt bankers were rich but dumb, so he decided to go into that sector. He had previously interned at the bank of Nova Scotia. From his time there, he deduced that banks liked to copy, and *"If there was a giant pile of gold sitting in the middle of the room and nobody was picking it up, they wouldn't pick it up, either."*

Musk decided to build an online bank with all the services, savings and checking accounts, brokerage, and insurance. A lot of people said it was not feasible. To them, he had the technology to build the bank, but he might not be able to maintain it because he would be dealing with people's finances.

Question to Ponder: Have you ever been in a situation where people doubted your ability to do something? How did you feel?

In total, Elon Musk fashion, "No," was not an option. While in Zip2, he started putting his plans to action. He talked to engineers and bank contacts to see who might be interested.

A month after Zip2 was sold to Compaq, Elon Musk announced his new company, "X.com." This company was to focus on online and email payment.

The team seemed like an all-star team. It included Harry Fricker and Christopher Payne.

In the beginning, there were personality clashes between the co-founders. At this point, it felt like Elon Musk had hacked Silicon Valley and become the dream; a dot-com millionaire. So, there was a lot of press around him, which didn't sit well with Fricker. Fricker felt that X.com was his opportunity to show the world what he was good at, which was banking. Also, Fricker wanted to run the company conventionally, so he found Elon Musk's visionary statements to be extra. Especially because the company was struggling to build anything.

Fricker threatened to take the company staff to build his own company if he was not made CEO. Elon Musk refused because he didn't like being blackmailed.

Question to Ponder: Have you ever been put in a position where it looked like you had no choice? What do you think Elon felt when he was being blackmailed by Fricker?

Since Elon Musk refused to let Fricker become CEO, he took employees and left. Five months after the company was created, more than half the employees were gone with a co-founder.

Question to Ponder: Have you ever encountered a difficult situation? How did you get out of it?

Elon Musk was sad, but he quickly got over it. He decided to hire new employees and look for more funding. He was able to get more employees through his speeches about the bigger picture. As the days passed, the company continued to hire more engineers, and the dream started to look feasible. By November, the company had gotten its banking and mutual funds license. They had even managed to get a partnership with Barclays. By Thanksgiving 1999, they had successfully created one of the world's first online banks, complete with FDIC insurance to back the bank accounts and three mutual funds for investors to choose from. Musk gave the engineers $100,000 of his own money to conduct their testing. On November 24, 1999, X.com went live to the public. Elon Musk was involved in every aspect of the launch. He *"stayed there forty-eight straight hours, making sure things worked."*

The bank tried out different concepts. For instance, customers got a $20 signing bonus cash card. They got $10 for every person they referred. They also dismissed overdraft charges and niggling fees.

In its first month, the company was booming. It had over 200 thousand subscribers. It was one of the first online banks to be federally insured.

As the company continued to boom, the investors decided that Elon Musk didn't have any experience, so they replaced him as the CEO with Bill Harris.

Question to Ponder: Have you ever been in a position where people felt you were not good enough and replaced you with another person? How did you feel? How do you think Elon Musk felt when he was replaced?

Soon the company had its competitors, Peter Thiel and Max Levchin of Confinity, whose software allowed users to swap money through the infrared ports of handheld palm pilots. They then started to focus on web payments and email payments with their service known as PayPal. Both companies were in a heated competition to match each other's features to attract more users. Elon Musk kept telling his employees to implement tactics that would give them an upper hand.

In March 2000, both companies decided that nothing was coming out of their rivalry, so x.com merged with Confinity to avoid competition. While PayPal had no cash reserves, X.com had a lot. This made Elon Musk the largest shareholder of the company.

With the merger of both companies, Elon Musk returned as the CEO. The companies tried hard to work together, but it was difficult. While Elon Musk kept trying to push X.com services, many people favored the service of PayPal.

Soon there was discord in the company. There was a major fight concerning the design of the company's infrastructure. Peter Thiel, and Max Levchin, the founders of Confinity, preferred the Linux software while Musk preferred Microsoft. The disagreement caused Thiel to resign. Levchin threatened to walk away. Elon was left to run a company that was broken.

Question to Ponder: Have you ever disagreed with someone? How did it feel?

Not long after, the company began to suffer from technological issues. The issues kept recurring, and the company had no business model. At least once a week, the website would collapse. The engineers were told to start building a new system. The engineers were distracted with building the new system, the old system became vulnerable to fraud. The company kept losing money. People started to question Musk's ability to actually make good decisions in the presence of a crisis.

Then, what happened next has been referred to as one of the nastiest coups in Silicon Valley. Some employees of X.com started to meet and contrive ways to get rid of Musk as the CEO. They decided to sell the idea to the board. They spoke about Thiel returning as the CEO. The board bought into the idea and decided to bring back Peter Thiel as the CEO.

At that time, Musk was on his honeymoon; all efforts to reach him were in vain. By the time his plane landed, Elon Musk had been replaced as the CEO by Peter Thiel.

When Musk heard of this action, he took the next plane to Palo Alto. He tried to talk to the board to rethink their decisions, but the company had moved on.

"It wasn't so much that I wanted to be CEO but more like, 'Hey, I think there are some pretty important things that need to happen, and if I'm not CEO, I'm not sure they are going to

happen.' But then I talked to Max and Peter, and it seemed like they would make these things happen. So then, I mean, it's not the end of the world." Musk said concerning the coup.

Some of his employees who were with him when X.com started were also surprised and angry by the coup.

Musk moved on and kept supporting Peter Thiel and Max Levchin. Thiel and Levchin rebranded the company like PayPal, and Musk kept his cool. He was not vindictive about it. He kept investing in the company, and soon he became the largest shareholder.

By mid-2001, most of Musk's influence in the company had faded. Then eBay came with the offer to buy PayPal. They agreed on $1.5 billion. Musk's share was $250 million, about $180 million after taxes.

This sale provided funds for Musk to invest in his lifelong dreams. However, the damage had been done to his reputation at this point. Eric Jackson, an early Confinity employee, wrote ***"The PayPal Wars: Battles with eBay, the Media, the Mafia, and the Rest of Planet Earth in 2004."***

He spoke about the company's journey, specifically the hard times. The book painted Musk as an egomaniacal, stubborn jerk who lacked critical decision-making skills. In turn, portrayed Thiel and Levchin as heroic geniuses.

Valleywag, the technology industry gossip site, added insult to injury as well and turned to bash Musk at every turn. The criticisms grew to the point that people started to doubt if Musk was a true co-founder of PayPal or had just ridden Thiel's coattails to a magical payday.

Question to Ponder: Have you ever been in a situation where someone tried really hard to destroy your reputation? If you were in Elon's shoes, how would you have reacted? Do you think it was good for Eric Jackson to keep painting Elon Musk black?

The book's tone and the blog posts goaded Musk, so in 2007, he wrote a 2,200-word email to Valleywag meant to set the record straight with his version of what happened.

He mentioned that Jackson was just a step above an intern who worshipped Peter Thiel. He further explained why he deserved his co-founder status, highlighting his role as its largest shareholder. The email also clarified that during his time as CEO, he hired a lot of the top talent elevating the company from sixty employees to several hundred and created a number of the company's most successful business ideas.

However, some of his employees mentioned that he badly handled the branding technology and fraud crisis. The idea that Musk was not a true co-founder of PayPal is a foolish take, and it has been supported by the other founders and the board.

It's important to note that Musk can be described as one of the internet banking and online payment pioneers. He made buying things from Amazon and eBay easier for all.

Space X

In 2001, Elon Musk joined the non-profit Mars Society. The society had plans to put a growth chamber for plants on Mars. Elon Musk was inspired by this project and wanted to fund the project himself.

When he clocked thirty in June that year, it started to dawn on him that he was no longer a child prodigy. Also, he was tired of the start-up life. He described it as *"eating glass and staring into the abyss."*

After PayPal had been ripped from him in a nasty way, he started to revisit his childhood fantasies of rocket ships and space travels. At that time, Elon and his wife Justine had moved to Los Angeles, California, which was the perfect city for aeronautics as it offered space.

Initially, Elon Musk was not sure about what he wanted to do, but since he was in the city of so many aeronautics companies, including NASA and the Air Force, he was certain he would be able to do something.

Question to Ponder: Have you ever jumped to do something you were not sure of? How did it feel?

Musk continued reading about rocket science, then joined the Mars Society. He impressed them in the first meeting with the society and donated to fund their research. Soon he became a member of the board.

Elon Musk had a good time in the Mars Society. Soon he started to think of doing things bigger than the Mars Society. So, he decided to send mice to Mars. They were to go and return and also procreate on the way. During the time this was happening, his friends did not know what to make of his mental health as Elon spent time fighting-off malaria and lost so much weight.

However, Elon Musk did not care. He became the butt of the jokes among his friends. One of his friends, Jeff Skoll, bought him a giant wheel of Le Brouère, a type of Gruyère. They were always making cheese jokes about him, and he laughed with them. He had a dream, and he was determined to achieve it.

Question to Ponder: Have you ever been made fun of because of what you wanted to achieve? Did you give up? If not, what kept you going?

Many people felt that Elon Musk was wasting resources on interplanetary travels for mice, but not Musk. He saw it as a way to inspire the public and revive the love for science and technology.

People were excited that a rich guy had money to throw around to fund a space project. This enthusiasm led Musk to invite industry space experts to help him develop his mice to space idea. After debating at a round table with those experts, they came to a consensus and decided to send plants to Mars instead. They called it Project Mars Oasis. The plan was to shoot a robotic greenhouse to Mars for this project. He wanted it to have windows that would open up briefly, take some soil from Mars to grow, and give oxygen to the Martian atmosphere. He also wanted the greenhouse equipped to transmit video information to earth. For Elon Musk, the project seemed feasible.

Many people had issues with Musk's budget. He wanted to spend about $20 million on the experiment, but many industry experts believed it was too small. According to them, he needed at least ten times his current budget to launch into space travels. There were also many engineering problems with the model Musk wanted. For instance, it would be difficult to keep anything warm enough to survive if the greenhouse had a window. If the plants didn't survive, then there would be another problem. Those problems needed to be solved.

This didn't faze Musk. He decided that he would get consultants and research how the greenhouse could be remodeled. So, he started to plan a trip to Russia. He wanted to determine how much the launch would cost and buy a refurbished intercontinental ballistic missile or ICBM to use as his launch vehicle.

His friends kept doubting his sanity. They had interventions, they kept compiling videos of rockets exploding, but it didn't change anything. Musk was still determined to work on space travel.

Question to Ponder: Have you ever been in a position where people tried their best to discourage you from achieving your dreams? How do you think Elon Musk felt from all the interventions?

When none of the interventions worked, they left Musk to do his own thing. Team Musk went to Russia three times in four months. Most of the meetings were futile. The other party didn't look like credible people. It felt like they just wanted to con a millionaire into giving out his money.

By the end of February 2002, the Musk team had not made progress. All their meetings with companies that could supply ICBMs and missiles were fruitless. The Russians were the only ones with missiles that fit Musk's budget. The team was dejected. One evening over drinks, Elon Musk says, *"Hey, guys, I think we can build this rocket ourselves."*

Jim Cantrell, a member of the Musk team who was present that evening, had to ask Elon if he had the resources to do so.

So, Elon brought out a spreadsheet; it had detailed costs of the materials needed to build, assemble, and launch a rocket. According to Musk's calculations, he could undercut existing launch companies by building a modest-sized rocket that would cater to a part of the market that specialized in carrying smaller satellites and research payloads to space. The spreadsheet also laid out the hypothetical performance characteristics of the rocket in fairly remarkable detail. It was really impressive.

So, Musk decided he would build cheaper rockets than the ones out there. People began speculating how he would fail and lose money. According to them, if he had just sent mice into space, he would have spent just twenty million. However, to build his rocket company, he would have had to put in hundreds of millions and still fail.

Musk had a secret weapon. That weapon was Tom Mueller. Tom grew up fixing broken devices and studying the way they worked. When he grew older, he started to make his own devices. He made a mock version of a space shuttle that could be attached to a rocket when he was twelve.

It was Mueller who helped Musk with the spreadsheet and cost metrics.

In June 2002, Elon Musk founded Space Exploration technologies. The company put engineers, computer scientists, machinists, and welders together in the same space. The office was in El Segundo, a suburb of Los Angeles.

For their first project, they called it Falcon 1, an ode to Star Wars. The plan was that the Falcon 1 would carry a 1,400-pound payload for $6.9 million. The deadline for the project was set for November 2003. Many of the space enthusiasts working on the project did not care; they were just happy that someone decided to take a faster and cheaper approach.

They started to research rocket explosions. They had the advantage of using the past mistakes of others to learn. Other people had invested billions in making rockets work, but

SpaceX was trying to make low-budget rockets. Many people didn't believe it could be done; not the team, though. Then, eBay bought PayPal, and with Musk's pay-out, he could afford to invest more in SpaceX. Things were looking good.

Then tragedy struck. Elon Musk's ten-week-old son, Nevada Alexander Musk, died. He suffered from what is known as infant death syndrome. His brain was deprived of oxygen; he was brain dead and kept on life support for three days before his parents made the heart breaking decision to take him off life support. It was a difficult time for Elon Musk and his wife, Justine. They were both grieving differently.

Question to Ponder: Have you ever lost someone close to you? How did you feel? How do you think Elon Musk and his wife felt about the death of their son?

After the death of Nevada, Musk threw himself into work. He started to work on the company's goals. He spoke to many aerospace contractors, but their pay was above what Misk was looking at. Those conversations left him discouraged. It didn't deter him, though; he assembled his all-star crew to start building. The crew included Tom Mueller, Chris Thompson, who was part of the team that created the Delta N and Titan rockets for Boeing, Steve Johnson, and Hans Koenigsmann, an aerospace engineer.

In SpaceX's first year, it had new employees weekly. Musk also employed Mary Beth Brown as his personal assistant. She could read Musk's moods and knew how to deal with them. She was an essential part of SpaceX and Tesla.

The company decided to work on a gas generator. It was a small machine that produced hot gas. When they tested the device, it worked. However, it left a cloud of black smoke in the air. They kept testing and tweaking; soon, the gas generator was to their liking.

When they started working on the Falcon 1, Mueller would often spot challenges with hardware and try to get replacement hardware that could correct the flaw. When it came to testing, the whole team was involved, including Elon Musk. He would join them with his nice clothes and *"Italian shoes."* At the end of the day, his clothes would be ruined and covered in epoxy.

While they worked on making the rocket, they had their first customer; they also announced that they were building another rocket, Falcon 5. To achieve that, they had to operate as a Silicon Valley start-up. They needed the best minds. When Musk found intelligent people, who could help with the course, he persisted in adding them to the team.

He was a very demanding boss to his employees, but he ensured that nothing prevented their productivity. Many of the employees were excited to be part of the team; they didn't care about Musk's demands.

The company had planned to launch the rocket in early 2004 but didn't. They realized that the Merlin engine was the most efficient of the engines built by the team. So, they started to test the machine to see if it would be approved for launch. By the fall of 2004, the engine had met all requirements.

Soon it was time to focus on the avionics of the rocket. This included the electronics for the navigation, communication, and overall management of the rocket. Things started to go wrong. Things that felt easy, like getting a flash storage drive to talk to the rocket's main computer, failed for reasons no one could explain. The software needed to manage the rocket also had its own issues. It went on for six months. Finally, in May, they completed a five-second burn on the launchpad at Vanderbilt Air Force Base.

The employees there who were supposed to help them with the launch made them feel unwelcomed, so they started to look for alternate places to launch. The new place they found was at Kwajalein Island. The SpaceX team didn't know a lot about launching, but they spent time figuring it out. By November 2005, they were ready to launch.

SpaceX launched the Falcon 1 on March 24, 2006. The rocket failed to reach the earth's orbit. However, it was awarded a Commercial Orbital Transportation Services program contract from NASA later that year. SpaceX said the rocket's failure to reach the earth's orbit was caused by a technician who failed to tighten a nut after working on the rocket the previous day.

http://allaboutbookseries.com/SpaceXLaunchFalcon1

A year later, SpaceX was ready to launch another Falcon 1. On March 27, March 2007, they launched it. The systems were normal, and it flew for three minutes before it crashed. It never reached the earth's orbit. The engineers figured out what happened quickly; the fuel was consumed. The remaining fuel started to move around the tank and slosh against the sides, so it exploded when the engine sucked air.

Question to Ponder: Have you worked hard on a project, and it got destroyed? How did you feel?

The failure dented SpaceX's ego. The company could only afford two more attempts at most. The failures didn't deter Elon Musk and pushed the team to do better.

After two failed launch attempts, the Falcon 1 finally reached the earth's orbit in 2008. It was a great feat as it was the first private liquid-fuel rocket to do so. Four years after the company's initial plan to launch the rocket, it was an excellent accomplishment.

SpaceX also received a $1.6 billion Commercial Resupply Services program contract from NASA for 12 flights of its Falcon 9 rocket and Dragon spacecraft to the International Space Station to replace the Space Shuttle after its 2011 retirement.

Question to Ponder: How do you think Elon Musk felt after successfully launching the rocket? If you were part of the team, how would you have felt at that moment?

The company continued to work towards its goal of making reusable rockets. The first part of this goal was achieved in 2015 when SpaceX landed the first stage of Falcon 9. They also landed an autonomous spaceport drone ship, an ocean-based recovery platform.

In 2017, SpaceX unveiled its next generation launch vehicle, a spacecraft system, Big Falcon Rocket, and was later renamed "Starship." It was to support all SpaceX launch service provider capabilities.

SpaceX also announced in 2018 a planned 2023 lunar circumnavigation mission, a private flight called dearMoon project.

In 2020, SpaceX launched its first crewed flight in the Dragon spacecraft. It became the first private company to place a person into orbit and dock a crewed spacecraft. It's the only spacecraft that can take humans to the space stations and carry cargoes to Earth.

SpaceX Launches Falcon 9 and Dragon Spacecraft

http://allaboutbookseries.com/SpaceXFalcon9

Elon Musk" by jdlasica is marked with CC BY 2.0.

Tesla

Tesla incorporated was founded in July 2003 by J.B. Straubel, Ian Wright, Martin Eberhard Marc Tarpenning, and Elon Musk as Tesla Motors. The company was named as a tribute to Nikola Tesla, a Serbian American inventor famous for making the AC generation and transmission technology.

J.B. Straubel graduated from Stanford University. Growing up, he had liked to fix things and check out what they were made of. In doing so, he revamped a totaled Porsche to an electric car, but when he noticed that the car couldn't go far, he transformed it into a hybrid car.

Years later, Straubel, along with some Stanford University students, discovered that Lithium batteries were powered to last longer. They were exploring solar panels when they realized this. So many devices like laptops were powered using Lithium-ion batteries. They started to wonder what they could achieve if they had a lot of Lithium-ion batteries connected. So, the idea was born.

The students had promised to join Straubel if he could raise funds to work on the project. Straubel spent time looking for investors, all to no avail. Then he was able to get a meeting with Elon Musk.

He announced his idea for Lithium-ion batteries that could power cars. Musk was excited. He had thought of electric vehicles but focused on ultracapacitors. Elon Musk promised to give Straubel $10 thousand out of the $100 thousand he needed.

Around that time, Martin Eberhard and Marc Tarpenning were playing with the idea of making cars powered with Lithium-ion batteries. Eberhard was interested in ways to stop global warming by finding alternatives to fuel. He thought of hydrogen gas fuel to power cars, but they could not do the work. He discovered all-electric cars from AC Propulsion from surfing the internet. So, he went to their store in LA and tried to convince them to make cars with Lithium-ion batteries rather than lead, but they refused. So, he decided to start his own company.

Eberhard started by building car prototypes, tweaking features here and there to see how they could affect the vehicle's performance. He realized that the technology favored lighter-weight sports cars. Tarpenning also discovered that people saw hybrid cars as another kind of status. Together, they decided to make luxury electric cars.

So, they started the company, but they needed funds to build the prototype. When they got a meeting with Elon Musk, Eberhard was excited. Musk was into the electric car project. So, he offered to invest $6.5 million. This made him the largest shareholder in the company.

After the meeting, Elon Musk called Straubel and urged him to meet with Tesla. He told them that he was building the battery pack they needed to power the car with funding from Elon Musk. He was hired after the appointment.

Elon Musk was active in the company, but he was not a part of the day-to-day operations. The day-to-day decision-making was done by Eberhard. The employees loved him for making quick critical decisions

Musk was very involved in the production of Tesla's roadster. He placed a high priority on comfort. He was particular about the Carbon Fiber body and electric sensors on the car.

By 2007, Tesla was making waves. The roadster was the fastest electric car. However, concerns were arising. There were problems with the transmission that could damage the vehicle. When the engineers started to work on it, they found fourteen other problems. There were also manufacturing issues in making batteries.

Musk heard about the production issues and became concerned about how Eberhard ran the company. He called a team to fix it. They also tried to protect their intellectual property. There were issues with the company's software; the whole thing was a mess.

The board started to doubt Eberhard's leadership abilities. This was also because he didn't disclose the magnitude of the problems to the board, and on his watch, some departments were neglected. So, the company demoted him, which he was not happy about. By the end of 2007, he left Tesla.

The board put Michael Marks as the CEO of the company. He put the company on the right track. Then he started to suggest that Tesla was an asset that could be done to larger car companies. This did not sit well with Elon Musk. Marks was soon replaced as the CEO.

In June 2009, Martin Eberhard sued Elon Musk for how he was ousted out of Tesla. The charges portrayed Musk as a bully. Musk retaliated. Both men settled their differences but still beefed each other privately.

Elon Musk started to get very involved with Tesla. He dealt with issues directly. He began to make the Tesla employees work hard. He would give speeches like "they would see their families a lot once the company went bankrupt." The employees began to see the Elon Musk, who the staff at SpaceX were acquainted with.

Question to Ponder: How do you think the employees working at Tesla felt?

Some of the employees started to get burnt out. Some of the initial members of the team left too.

The company had to find a way to convince investors to put in more money during a financial crisis where so many car companies were filing for bankruptcy. He invested all his cash which accrued up to $200 million, into the business. He borrowed $200,000 from friends and lived on them for a long time. He mentioned that he invested *"his last cent into the business"* in a divorce case."

He could have sold some of his Tesla stocks, but he didn't.

Question to Ponder: If you were Elon Musk and your business needed cash, would you have sold stocks or funded the company? Do you think Elon Musk made an intelligent decision putting his last cent in the business?

Tesla finally got its well-deserved break in 2012 when it started shipping the Tesla Model S. It shocked the automobile industry. First, it goes more than 300 miles on a single charge. It could reach 60 miles per hour in 4.2 seconds. If you used the optional rear-facing seats in the back for kids, the car could seat up to seven people. It also had two trunks. It was a different type of luxury. What made it better was that Tesla didn't sell to salespeople. You had to buy directly from the company. Clients also had the option of pickup and could arrange a tour of the Tesla office in Silicon Valley for them and their families. The automobile had also managed to do away with traditional mass-produced car problems like oil changes and tune-ups. The company was customer-based; if there were an issue with the car, Tesla would come to pick it up and give the customer a loaner while it repaired the Model S. They could also fix glitches in the car's system by making an update on the car's software to correct the malfunctions. This means that the car owners didn't have to bring their vehicles to the Tesla office to fix them. They could be sleeping, and Tesla was fixing glitches by updating the car's software.

By doing this, the company turned the Model S into a car that got better with each update.

A year after the Model S went on sale, Tesla recorded $562 million in quarterly income. It was huge. People were comparing it to the iPhone of cars. The business was valuable; the goods were luxury.

Question to Ponder: How do you think Elon Musk and the Tesla staff felt when the Tesla Model S started to make waves in the automobile industry?

So many automobile companies did not see Tesla becoming big. First, it was an American car company, and they were focusing on electric cars. To the mainstream automobile companies, Tesla was not a threat. They believed it was a bored Silicon Valley millionaire pumping money till he could no longer afford to. Therefore, the success of Tesla was a shock to them. They could not believe that an American car company worked on electric cars successfully.

Question to Ponder: How do you think mainstream automobile companies felt when Tesla finally made sales in the market?

There were so many controversial statements about Elon Musk being the true founder of Tesla. Whatever people say, the truth is there would be no Tesla if Elon Musk had not poured money into it.

Tesla's 2012 Model S

http://allaboutbookseries.com/TeslaModel5

Elon Musk also won different awards for the design of the Tesla roadster.

Recently, Elon Musk has open-sourced Tesla technology so other companies could benefit from it. It is so impressive.

Question to Ponder: Do you think Elon Musk made a good decision by open-sourcing Tesla technology?

SolarCity and Tesla Energy

Brothers Lyndon and Peter Rive founded SolarCity in 2006. Elon Musk gave the initial concept and capital to start the business. The business became successful, and by 2013, it became the second-largest provider of solar power in the U.S.

The company built an advanced production facility in Buffalo, New York. The building is triple the size of the largest solar plant in the United States. The construction started in 2014 and ended in 2017. Elon Musk influenced the construction of the building.

Tesla bought SolarCity in 2016 for over $2 billion. They merged it with their battery-producing department. Together, they formed a new subdivision, Tesla energy.

Tesla's stocks dropped by more than 10 percent when the deal was announced. The board was incensed. What happened was that SolarCity energy was facing liquidity, and the shareholders of Tesla were not informed. They got offended and decided to sue Musk and the directors of Tesla. The shareholders claimed that the purchase was just for Elon Musk's benefit.

Question to Ponder: How do you think Elon Musk felt about the lawsuit? Do you think the shareholders were right in making that decision?

In a court deposition held in June 2019, Musk disclosed that the company reallocated every possible employee from the solar division to work on the Tesla Model 3, and *"as a result, solar suffered."*

This was not disclosed to shareholders. Court documents have also confirmed that Musk was aware of the company's liquidity issues.

The directors of Tesla were able to settle their case, but Musk is still in court as the sole defender.

SolarCity and Tesla

http://allaboutbookseries.com/WhatHappenedToSolarCity

Neuralink

Elon Musk founded Neuralink, a neurotechnology company, in 2016. This company was founded to integrate the human brain with artificial intelligence. To achieve this, they decided to create devices that could be embedded in the human brain to facilitate its merging with machines.

How Neuralink Works

http://allaboutbookseries.com/HowNeuralinkWorks

Elon Musk described the device as *"a Fitbit in your skull."* It has been said that the device can cure paralysis, deafness, blindness, and other disabilities. However, these claims have been criticized by many neuroscientists.

The Latest Neuralink News

http://allaboutbookseries.com/Neuralink2022

The Boring Company

Elon Musk founded "The Boring Company" in 2016. The company was founded to construct tunnels; they discussed with regulatory bodies. They constructed a 30-foot wide, 50-foot long, and 15-foot deep "test trench" on the premises of SpaceX's offices as it required no permits to do so.

Check Out The Boring Company's Tunnel

http://allaboutbookseries.com/BoringCompanyTunnel

They did a publicity stunt and sold 20,000 novelty flamethrowers in 2018. They got the idea from the Spaceballs movie. Though they were not actual flamethrowers, people were excited to buy them. They also sold caps.

Maurizio Pesce from Milan, Italia CC by 2.0

Elon Musk's Relationship and Marriage

Elon Musk met his first wife, Justine Wilson, while they were still students at Queen's University in Ontario, Canada. On their first date, Elon invited her to go for ice cream, but she opted to stay in to study. Elon showed up at her door with two chocolate chips ice cream cones dripping down his hands. It was such a sweet gesture. A while later, Elon Musk transferred to Wharton, University of Pennsylvania, and he continued to send Justine roses.

Question to Ponder: How do you think Justine felt when she received the roses?

The couple later went their separate ways and reconnected when Elon started building Zip2. Justine was working on her first novel too. The author has revealed that the tech businessman won her heart by giving her his credit card to buy whatever book she wanted. Sweet!

They got married in 2000.

The couple moved to Los Angeles after Musk was fired from PayPal. They also lost their ten-week-old son, Nevada Musk. It was a tough time for the couple. Justine wanted to grieve openly, while Musk wanted to be left alone. He didn't see the point in grieving openly.

Not long after, the couple started rounds of intro video fertilization. They had five sons from the process. A pair of twins and a pair of triplets.

In 2010, Elon Musk mentioned that his children are *"the love of my life."*

The couple divorced in 2008.

Question to Ponder: How do you think the couple felt going their separate ways?

Shortly after the divorce, Elon Musk started dating British actress Talulah Riley. The duo got married in 2010. Riley was also close to Justine Wilson.

Two years after Riley and Musk got married, rumors of their divorce started to go round. It became official when Musk confirmed it via Twitter. He tweeted, *"It was an amazing four years. I will love you forever. You will make someone very happy one day."*

The couple remarried the following year. Musk filed for divorce again but withdrew it.

Finally, in 2016, Talulah Riley filed for divorce, and it was finalized in 2016. The duo is still close even after the divorce. She told People, *"We still see each other all the time and take care of each other."* She also made an appearance during the Rolling Stone profile of Elon Musk.

In 2016, Elon Musk started dating Amber Heard, the female lead of Marvel's Aquaman. The duo broke up because of differences in their busy schedules.

About the relationship, Musk has mentioned that *"still friends, remain close and love one another, and who knows what the future holds."* He later told Rolling Stone that he *"was really in love, and it hurt bad."*

Elon Musk and Amber Heard

http://allaboutbookseries.com/ElonMuskAmberHeard

In 2018, Elon Musk started dating Canadian singer Grimes. The couple met on Twitter when Musk was planning to make an AI joke about the Rococo Basilisk character in her "Flesh Without Blood" video. The couple showed up at the MET Gala together.

Grimes Flesh Without Blood Music Video

http://allaboutbookseries.com/GrimesFleshWithoutBlood

Musk admitted in the Wall Street Journal that he loves Grimes because of her *"wild fae artistic creativity and hyperintense work ethic."*

In 2020, Grimes announced that she was expecting a baby with Elon Musk. On May 4, 2020, Elon Musk took to his Twitter and announced the birth of their baby. He wrote, *"Mom & baby all good,"* The baby was named *"X Æ A-Xii Musk,"* seemingly pronounced *"X Ash A-12."*

They moved to Texas in December to be close to SpaceX facilities.

However, in September 2021, Elon Musk announced that he and Grimes had broken up. He mentioned that their busy work schedules caused the breakup. While he needs to be in Texas or traveling around for work, Grimes' work is solely based in LA.

Elon Musk's Dating List

http://allaboutbookseries.com/ElonMuskDatingList

Elon Musk's Other Projects

Hyperloop

Elon Musk proposed a high-speed vacuum train for passengers and freight in 2013. He called it a hyperloop. The train uses the design of tubes, pods, and terminals. He deployed engineers from Tesla and SpaceX to work on it.

The design has been published in a white paper. Transport analysts have said that if the cost is the same as that published and it's technologically feasible, it will be the cheapest form of transport.

It uses magnets in a tube to transport. The whole idea behind it is brilliant.

In 2017, Musk announced that he had gotten verbal approval from the government to build a hyperloop from New York to DC, stopping at Philadelphia and Baltimore. However, in 2021, the details of this project were removed from the website of The Boring Company.

http://allaboutbookseries.com/ElonMuskHyperloop

He has made the hyperloop project an open source, so people can work on it. Hyperloop companies are working on the best magnets to use for the tube. They are also developing other hyperloop technologies. One of them is Virgin Hyperloop.

Open AI Non-profit

Elon Musk started a non-profit for artificial intelligence research. It aims at developing artificial intelligence that is safe for humans. The focus is to make sure that large corporations do not own all the superintelligence systems in the world.

However, in 2018, Elon Musk left the board to prevent any controversies that might arise from his role as the CEO of Tesla. The company became increasingly involved in AI through Tesla autopilot.

Question to Ponder: How do you think Elon Musk felt leaving the board of the AI non-profit?

Appearance on Joe Rogan's Podcast

Elon Musk can also be found in the media space. One of these is his appearance on Joe Rogan's podcast on September 6, 2018. The host of the podcast, Joe Rogan, is known for his controversial statements, using racial slurs, and even spreading misinformation about COVID19.

On the podcast, he spoke about different topics ranging from The Boring Company's mercy to fixing LA traffic by building tunnels to Elon being an Alien. They talked about various things for two hours; it was interesting to watch.

Things took a turn when Elon sampled Rogan's cigar, tobacco laced with cannabis. The media turned the story around, and *"it became a story about Musk's growing instability."*

Tesla's stocks dropped after that podcast incident. It coincided with Tesla's Vice President of Worldwide finance leaving the company. There were assumptions that the use of cannabis might affect SpaceX's contracts with the government.

About the whole situation, Elon Musk mentioned that he doesn't smoke cannabis, and anybody watching the podcasts could notice that.

Elon Musk on Joe Rogan Experience

http://allaboutbookseries.com/ElonMuskJoeRogan

Elon Musk's Charity

Like most billionaires, Elon Musk has been involved in charity. He is the head of the Musk Foundation. A charity set up to donate solar power energy systems in disaster areas and support research and educational goals.

Since it was founded in 2002, the foundation has made 350 donations. Most of these donations are to scientific research and educational non-profits.

A lot of people have criticized the foundation for the small number of donations it has made. As of 2018, the foundation had given out $25 million, of which half went to Musk's AI non-profit.

In 2012, Musk took the giving pledge. He promised to give the majority of his wealth to charitable causes during his lifetime or in his will.

Even with all his philanthropic deeds, Musk still has a Forbes philanthropy score of 1 as of 2020. Interesting, isn't it? Well, this is because Elon Musk has not given away up to one percent of his net worth

Elon Musk granted the X prize foundation $15 million for innovation in addressing illiteracy. He also donated $100 million to improve carbon removal in the environment.

As of November, 2021, he donated $5.7 billion worth of Tesla shares to charity.

Elon Musk's Awards and Achievements

For a man as great as Elon Musk, he can't have gone through his career and risen to the richest man in the world without having earned some achievements.

He is widely appreciated for his efforts to combat climate change. Bill Gates even said that *"what Elon did with Tesla is one of the greatest contributions to climate change anyone's ever made."*

Musk has received a lot of praise for his efforts in the environment and space travel. Here is a list of Elon Musk's awards and achievements.

2006- He was part of the United States National Academy of Sciences Aeronautics and Space Engineering Board.

He was also awarded the Global Green 2006 product design award for his design of the Tesla Roadster.

2007- Inc magazine awarded him the Entrepreneur of the Year award for 2007 for his work on Tesla and SpaceX.

Another award he won was the Index Design award for his design of the Tesla Roadster.

2008- He was recognized for his design of the Falcon 1, the first privately developed liquid-fuel rocket to reach orbit. For this achievement, he won a George Low award for "the most outstanding contribution in the field of space transportation in 2007/2008."

He also won a National Conservation Achievement award for his efforts at Tesla and SolarCity.

He also won the National Space Society's Von Braun Trophy in 2008/2009; the trophy was given for the leadership of "the most significant achievement in space."

2010- He was listed as one of the 100 people who influenced the world.

He was also awarded the most sought-after award in air and space. The highest achievement in that sector; the FAI Gold Space Medal, which he won for designing the first privately developed rocket to reach orbit by Fédération Aéronautique Internationale.

Esquire magazine named him one of the 75 people in the 21st century who positively influenced the world.

For inventing the Falcon 9 and Dragon spacecraft, Kitty Hawk Foundation recognized him as the leading aviation legend in 2010.

2011- He was listed on Forbes' list "America's 20 Most Powerful CEOs 40 And Under."

Later in June, he won an award for US$250,000 Heinlein Prize for Advances in Space Commercialization.

2012- Elon Musk won the Royal Aeronautical Society's gold medal. This is the highest award of the Society.

2013- Fortune named him the year's businessperson for his work at Tesla and SolarCity.

2014- At the annual gala of the Explorers Club, Musk won the President's Award for Exploration and Technology.

He was also commemorated with an Edison Achievement Award. It was given for his "commitment to innovation throughout his career."

2015- He got an honorary Yale doctorate in engineering and technology.

He also got an honorary membership from IEEE.

2016- He was listed as one of the "Top 10 Business Visionaries Creating Value for the World." Mark Zuckerberg was also on that list by Business Insider.

2017- He won the award for the Oslo Business for Peace.

2018- He was ranked as the 25th most powerful person globally on Forbes list.

He was also listed among Times 100 most influential people in the world.

2019- He won the Starmus Festival's Stephen Hawking Medal for Science Communication.

He was also listed on Forbes's list of "Most Innovative Leaders of 2019."

2020- He was listed as one of the Top 100 most influential Africans by New African magazine.

He also won the Axel Springer award in 2020.

And he was ranked first on Fortune Magazine's top businessmen of the year in 2020.

2021- Bloomberg named Elon Musk the richest person in the world.

Forbes also listed him as #1 on Forbes billionaire list.

He was named Person of the Year for his efforts to advance the world's auto industry towards EVs by Financial Times.

He was awarded a spot on the Newsweek Hall of Fame for his revolution in the Auto and Space Industry.

He was also named Times Magazine person of the year.

2022- National Academy of Engineering revealed that Elon Musk was awarded as one of their newly peer-elected members. This award is considered to be among the highest professional recognition accorded to an engineer *"for breakthroughs in the design, engineering, manufacturing, and operation of reusable launch vehicles and sustainable transportation and energy systems."*

Question to Ponder: Did you feel inspired by Elon Musk's story? What lessons did you learn from him?

Elon Musk's Timeline

June 28, 1971- Elon Musk was born in Pretoria, South Africa.

1980- Elon Musk's parents got divorced.

1981- Elon Musk became interested in programming and started to teach himself how to code.

January 12, 1983- The source code for Elon's blaster game, which he wrote as a twelve-year-old child, was published in a magazine. He sold it for $500.

June 1989- Elon Musk moved to Canada at the age of seventeen.

1992- Elon Musk studied at the University of Pennsylvania, getting a double bachelor's degree in economics and physics.

1995- Elon Musk started the Zip2 company with Kimbal, his younger brother.

February 1999- Zip2 was sold to Compaq for $307 million.

March 1999- Elon Musk founded X.com with Harry Fricker and Christian Payne.

2000- X.com merged with Confinity to form PayPal. Elon Musk also married his first wife, Justine Wilson, who he met in Ontario, while they were both students at Queen's University.

October 2000- Elon Musk got fired from his job as the CEO of PayPal.

He also lost his ten-week-old son, Alexander Nevada Musk.

Early 2001- Elon Musk started forming the concept of the Mars Oasis along with the Mars Society.

In October 2001, Musk started his Russian travels to search for a ballistic missile or ICBM for space travel.

2002- The Musk Foundation was founded

February 2002- Elon Musk decided to build his own company to build affordable rockets.

May 2002- Elon Musk started SpaceX to build rockets. He was the CEO and CTO of the company.

October 2002- eBay bought PayPal for $165 million.

July 2003- Tesla was incorporated in the U.S.

2004- Elon Musk and his wife welcomed a set of twins.

He also joined Tesla as a member of the board.

March 24, 2004- Falcon 1 was launched, but it failed to reach the earth's orbit.

2006- Elon Musk and his wife welcomed a set of triplets through IVF.

He gave his cousins the concept to start their company and also financed it. The company was SolarCity.

SpaceX started to get contracts from government agencies like NASA.

2007- Elon Musk became the CEO and product architect of Tesla.

March 27, 2007- SpaceX attempted another launch of Falcon 1. It flew for three minutes before it crashed.

2008- Elon Musk and his first wife Justine got a divorce.

Falcon 1 reached the earth's orbit.

2010- Elon Musk married Talulah Riley, an English actress.

The Musk Foundation donated a 25-kW solar power system to the official South Bay Community Alliance's Hurricane Response Center from SolarCity.

2011- Elon Musk revealed his plans to send humans to Mars to the public.

2012- Tesla and SolarCity collaborated to make better batteries for electric cars.

SpaceX Dragon docked on the ISS.

2013- SolarCity became the second-largest solar service provider in the United States.

Elon Musk also revealed his concept for hyperloop transportation through reduced pressure in tubes.

2014- Elon Musk announced that Tesla technology would be open-sourced, so anyone can use it.

June 17, 2014- SolarCity started to build its production facility in New York.

2015- Elon Musk made a Simpson cameo appearance titled "The Musk who fell to Earth."

January 2015- He held a hyperloop design competition.

November 2015- Elon Musk made a cameo appearance on The Big Bang Theory.

December 2015- Elon Musk created OpenAI.

2016- Elon Musk started dating Amber Heard, the female lead of Aquaman.

Tesla also acquired SolarCity.

During this time, The Boring Company was founded.

Elon Musk and Max Hodak also co-founded Neuralink.

Musk acquired 54% of SpaceX stocks, giving him 78% voting shares.

He also revealed plans to colonize Mars.

2017- They started to run a test for Hyperloop.

2018- Elon Musk left the board of OpenAI to avoid clashes with Tesla.

The Boring Company sold 20,000 flamethrowers and 50,000 caps.

July 2018- He built a rescue Pod to help with Tham Luang cave rescue, but it was never used.

He appeared on Joe Rogan's podcast.

2019- Elon Musk went to China for the building of the new Tesla giant factory in Shanghai

2021- Elon Musk donated $5.7 billion worth of Tesla shares to charity.

He also donated $100 million for Xprize Carbon removal.

References

General

Elon Musk by Ashlee Vance

https://www.businessinsider.com/elon-musk-relationships-2017-11?amp

Introduction

https://www.britannica.com/biography/Elon-Musk

Early Childhood

Elon Musk by Ashlee Vance

Education

Elon Musk by Ashlee Vance

https://www.britannica.com/biography/Elon-Musk

Business

https://www.investopedia.com/articles/personal-finance/061015/how-elon-musk-became-elon-musk.asp

Space X

https://www.spacex.com/

Tesla

https://www.tesla.com/

https://www.cnbc.com/amp/2017/04/27/the-crucial-decision-teslas-elon-musk-had-to-make-when-he-was-broke.html

Timeline

https://www.techtimes.com/amp/articles/262120/20210628/elon-musk-turns-50-heres-a-timeline-of-his-achievements.htm

Final Surprise Bonus

Hope you've enjoyed this biography of Elon Musk

We always like to give more than we get, so I'd like to give you one final bonus.

Do me a favor, if you enjoyed this book, please leave a review on Amazon.

It'll help get the word out so more kids can find out more about Elon Musk!

If you do, I'll send you one of my most cherished video collection – Free:

Ultimate Collection of Links to Elon Musk's YouTube Videos!

You won't be able to say you know Elon Musk until you watch these videos!

Here's how to claim your free videos:

1. Leave a review right away -

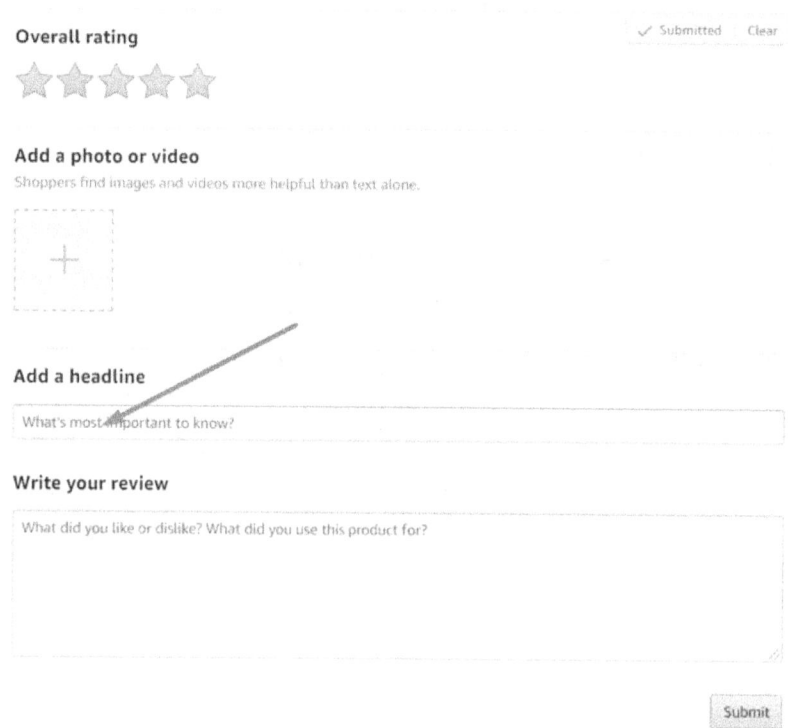

2. Send a screenshot of your review to: reviews@allaboutbookseries.com with the subject line: All About Elon Musk Review

3. Receive your free video collection – *"Ultimate Collection of Links to Elon Musk's YouTube Videos! " – immediately*!